Cloud Mountain

William Doreski

ISBN: 978-81-19654-67-3

First Edition: 2024
Rs. 200/-

Cyberwit.net
HIG 45 Kaushambi Kunj, Kalindipuram
Allahabad - 211011 (U.P.) India
http://www.cyberwit.net
Tel: +(91) 9415091004
E-mail: info@cyberwit.net

Printed at Repro India Limited.

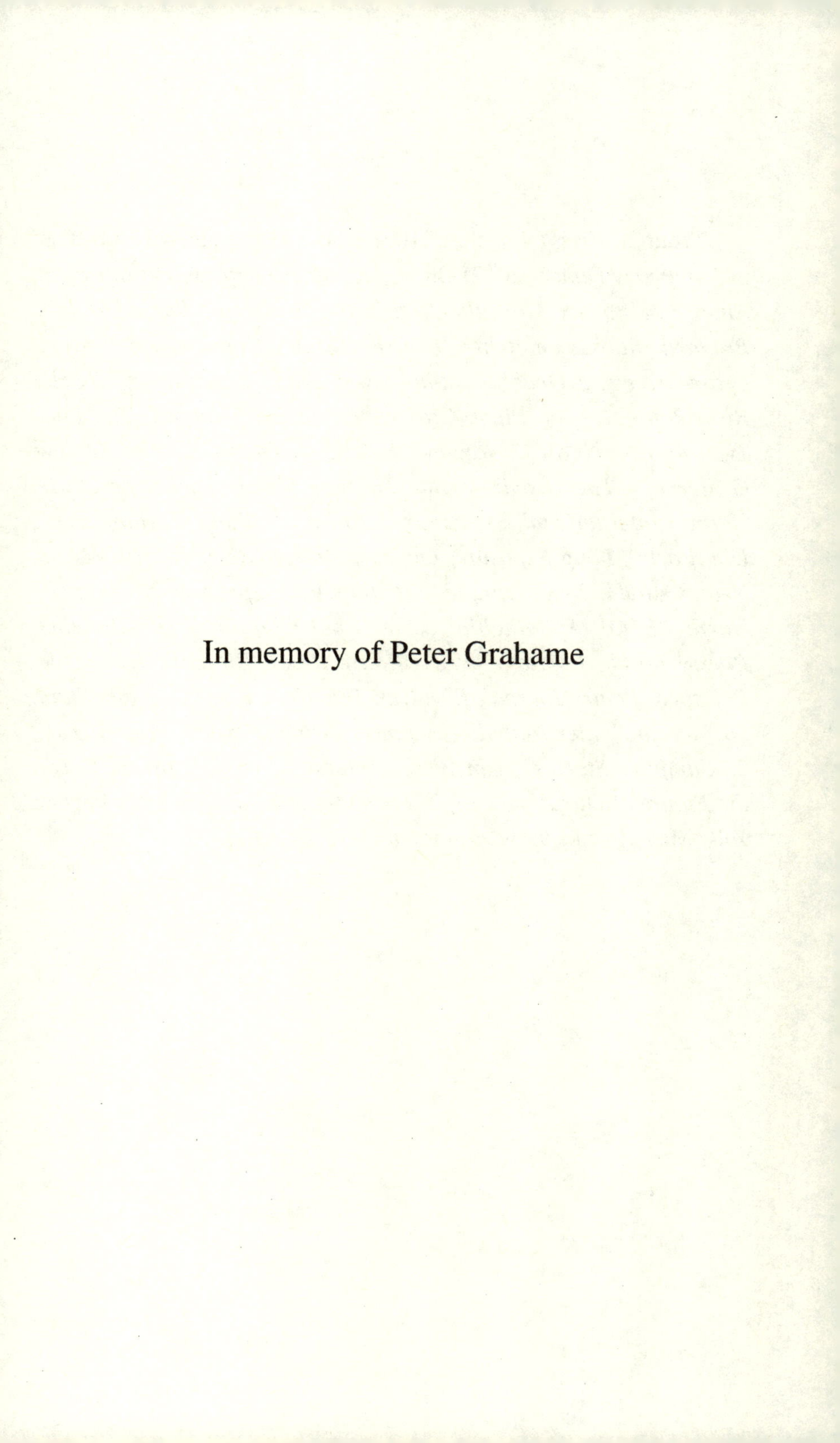

In memory of Peter Grahame

"Your Sea Bass" won the 2010 Aesthetica Prize and was published in *June Snow Dance* (2012).Other poems have appeared in *Abridged, American Poetry Monthly, Antithesis, Arboreal, Backchannels, Barzakh, Book of matches, Bruiser, Canto, Caper, Cascades and Crosscurrents: A Quabbin Anthology, Ceilidh, Cerebration, Charles River Journal, Club Plum, Crosswinds, Ethos, Fishbowl, The Five-Two, 400 and Falling Review, Foxglove, Garfield Lake Review, Glittermob, The Gravity of the Thing, Halfway Down the Stairs, Harvest International, The Helix, I-70 Review, Kelp, Levitate, Little Dog Poetry, Long Exposure, Lunaris, Mohave River Review, Moria, Neon Garden, New Critique, Nightingale & Sparrow, No Contact, North / South Appalachia, One Hand Clapping, The Phoenix, Poetry Porch, Porridge, Press Pause Press, Project Nightingale, Pulsebeat Poetry Journal, Revolver, The River, River & South, Slant, Solstice: a Winter Anthology, spoKe, Swing, Timada's Diary, TMP 2: Campfire Stories, Twin Bird, Underscore, Voices of the Earth: the Future of Our Planet III, The Wondrous Real, Worcester Review, Yolk.* Many thanks to the editors of these journals.

Contents

Your Sea Bass

At the end of India Wharf
before they built the aquarium
you dropped a line, bait and sinker,
for the first time in your life.

The harbor light ignited
your blonde expression. The old men
who fished there every afternoon
applauded when you hooked a bass.

As I netted the slippery muscle
you cried for fear the hook hurt.
Behind us the custom house clock
aligned its hands for six PM.

Traffic on the Central Artery,
a green steel monstrosity,
sizzled in the heavy June heat.
You stared your fish in the eye,

made mouth motions like its own.
It felt like ten pounds in the net,
more meat than the old men had caught
all week. Hot wind ruffed the water,

striking an enormous shade of blue.
Unhooking the fish as gingerly
as I'd unhook you or myself,
I tipped the net and poured the sea bass

back into its environment.
The old men cheered as the creature
splashed a V for victory
with the fork of its powerful tail.

Profiled against the drifting
of the sculpted harbor islands,
you smiled so absolutely
I mistook you for the horizon.

2-22-22

No woodpeckers pulping suet
this winter, no juncos or finches
throbbing at the sunflower feeder.
Bad to find the woods depleted,
the river sullen under ice.

February is a tombstone engraved
with cruel numerical sentiments.
You break the ice on the birdbath
but no flutter or chirp responds.
I scan the meadow with powerful

binoculars, sorting and filing
every frost-brown stalk and twig.
The tragic silence embalms us
in colors that barely register.
We should have lived urban lives

without expecting birdsong
to shore up our timid phonics.
We should wake to the song of trash
trucks prowling the boulevards,
and spend our winter afternoons

perking in the art museums,
where painted scenes overlap
those we've kept since childhood.
Now our back yard merges
with forest spangled by dawn.

We could follow our tracks and find
the local bear asleep in the rocks
with rump exposed to the sunlight
and occasional but angry storms.
We hibernate inside ourselves

and ignore the absence of birds
except on days like this when
we stroll in unseasonable warmth
and try not to count ourselves
among the urgently missing.

Sea Voices

You arrive in a straight line.
Your bangles and dangles follow,
chattering like miniature parrots.

Your leather luggage suggests
turtles basking on weedy rocks.
Your smile levels the hired help.

I found the corpse of your latest
lover washed up on the beach.
The great white sharks rejected him

after sampling his bitter flesh.
If you were the yachting type
I'd say you pushed him overboard,

but you get seasick just watching
the combers roll up on the sand.
The hotel is a massive cake

decorated by expert bakers.
You'd like to slice off a slab
and devour and digest it

with cunning giggles and smirks.
Tonight at dinner you'll explain
yourself with allusions to books

you know I'm too old to read.
Your jewelry will fail to dazzle
because I prefer my minerals

uncut and fresh from bedrock.
But later from your wrought iron
balcony we'll listen to sea-life

plot against evolution, squid
with their thin voices, crabs grumbling,
whales and dolphins speaking plain

serviceable English. We won't hear
the great white sharks complaining
about your lover's toxic flavor.

We'll hear something deeper groaning
in dark so absolute the moon
can't tempt it to rise and show itself

in primal spectrums you'd envy.
You've never been naked enough
to discover them in yourself.

An Arson of the Spirit

Fire has ruined the bedrock chapel
monks haunted for hundreds of years.
The Cambrian granite walls
remain rigid enough to resist
nuclear war, but the famous
stained glass windows liquesced
and the wood truss roof collapsed.
I nose through the rubble in hopes
of collecting a relic
of puddled gold. But firefighters
have already combed the mess
for human remains and surely
bagged everything of value. No one
died, no priest has said mass
for twenty years, the structure
more a museum than a church.
I like the scorched blank walls,
the cinders of the oak altar,
the smears of colored glass beneath
gaping window-holes. No monks
survive to mourn the ruin.
Their order disbanded after
half a dozen girls disappeared
and the corpse of one turned up
with vampire bites on her groin.
The cardinal hushed up the crime
but someone torched the chapel
two decades later because
the grief hung over the town

like a smut of sulfur dioxide.
At last I uncover something—
a tiny silver cross unscathed
by the heat. Not a crucifix
but a simple geometric shape
to accept a suffering Jesus.
Protestants prefer the living Christ,
but whoever torched this structure
wanted to bury the history
that so poignantly inflames us—
the granite walls five hundred
million years old but grinning
as if created fresh this morning
when this godless day evolved.

Tracing Dinosaur Tracks

After tracing dinosaur tracks
that snuffed out at the tide line
I awaken to snow showers
falling through certain organs
I only use when asleep.

Today will go like this: slick
back roads, coffee shop coffee
with a cranberry muffin crumbling,
a bag of groceries, a visit
to the bank with the green logo,

an afternoon reading paperbacks
in propane heat, a distance
unfolding like a loveless letter,
more snow showers weeping down
through the fey embrace of pines.

Most of my friends died years ago,
faces adrift in pearly vapors.
On the phone with the few survivors
I find my voice too numb to express
the texture of localized snowfall.

Such erasure troubles without
surprising me. Think of dusty
storefronts, rooms without views.
I've inhabited such places longer
than most people want to live.

Maybe the tracks I followed
were my own from a far era.
Maybe I should have lingered
at the tideline where this world
and that one interact with joy.

Glass Man

Made of glass this morning,
I'm pleased that anyone can see
through me to the landscape beyond.

Being so fragile I take great care
walking up the post office steps.
Standing in line I avoid

bumping old ladies clutching
parcels intended for grandkids.
The day sighs many great sighs.

It expects me to understand why
I'm made of glass this morning,
instead of rising in a fist

of stainless steel. The river
brims at the post office window.
It also is glass this morning.

If I stepped on it, tried to walk
its naked water, we'd collapse
into each other's shy embrace,

subject and verb uniting.
I reach the window to buy a stamp
but the clerk looks right through me

to the next person in line.
I cough to get his attention
but something inside me cracks

and I have to step aside and clutch
myself to myself to avoid
shattering all over the floor.

I'll mail my letter tomorrow
when I've reverted to simple flesh.
Today I'd better lie down somewhere

in the shade so I don't start a fire.
Somewhere in the damp old forest
where no one will step on me,

my utter transparency
plain as an artist's model,
too slick to exhibit shame.

Consequent Rhythm

A house of dusty bedrooms.
No one's ever home. Braving
the vacancy, I step inside
to face the wind blowing down
long wainscoted corridors
where detached voices whisper.

A few sparrows trapped inside
flutter through the opened doorway.
They'll find the season depleted
in depressing shades of brown.
I enter a bedroom at random
and find a Rolex watch ticking

on a table with a book facedown.
Collected Poems of Wallace Stevens.
I read a couplet: "Is it bad
to have come here / And have found
the bed empty?" I reject
such consequent rhythm, the film

of filtered light sculpting a form
in the rumpled sheets. I resist
stealing the watch and tempting fate
by brandishing an obvious crime.
In the next bedroom the scent
of a couple coupling lingers.

On the floor, a bloodstained pillow.
I don't want to picture the drama,
so withdraw in a huff and sigh.
At the end of the corridor
tinsel drapes a lamp that if lit
would shiver and crack the spectrum.

I try to reason my way out,
but a blank wall saddens me
and the rhythm of the afternoon
forbids retreat. The wispy voices
struggle to gather strength enough
to shout me down in my tracks.

Another Brave New World

You read that France has shattered
into a thousand small islands,
each with a church, school, and jail.

You say that a Welsh village fielded
a winning Super Bowl team
composed of retired miners.

You note that the spy balloons
from China now deliver takeout.
In this same global spirit

Congress now meets in Cancun
because the food is spicy-hot
and appeals to avid debaters.

Martyrs perform in Carnegie Hall,
demons commandeer the subways.
We should cancel our flight to Paris

and stop betting on football.
We'll live on takeout and resolve
to vote by mail and take the bus

when we must get to City Hall
to confer with our feckless mayor.
France must purchase a thousand

ferryboats to service itself
so we should buy shipbuilding stock.
What if we move to Wales and live

in the shade of heaped mine tailings?
What if we visit our Congress
in the Yucatan and shake their hands

and sample the local cuisine?
By now the spiders have eaten
half of our elected officials,

while the rest have gone into hiding
as if one could hide from spiders.
Maybe France has begun to heal,

the islands drifting and bumping
and gradually rejoining. Surely
we too are drifting. In the dusty

streets of Manhattan we find ourselves
duplicated in all we meet,
tempers unsheathed and hissing.

Temple of Mystic Gestures

The sprawl of shadow across the slope reminds me to lie down in the road to be run over at your convenience. Thank you for the tire tracks across my midsection. They didn't hurt, but the weight of your little electric car softened some of my favorite organs. Don't worry: they'll heal. And if they don't, I'll self-refer to the neighborhood temple of mystic gestures, where strange gods deploy with little giggles and sneers.

Meanwhile gunshots riot in the forest as deer hunters plug each other. They laugh and smash beer cans on their foreheads. The beer is still in the cans, though, and the hunters knock themselves senseless. What a violent world we've created—my dented torso, the concave foreheads and shot-riddled carcasses of hunters, the shadows warping the hillside. You reverse your little car and back right over me again, hoping I'll burst like a pinata. I won't. I've toughened in the sloped November light, my skin tanned and fine-grained enough to contain and waterproof me against even your slyest intentions.

Ingesting the Moon

Every time you swallow the moon
you retch it up like a hairball.
Then you fling the slimy disc

into the sky and hope it sticks
to reassure the public that myth
hasn't failed them. It's so small

that tales of astronauts landing
on its rough surface make no sense.
They'd have to be germ-sized to walk,

play golf and look down on Earth
from such a modest aerie.
Many people realize the truth—

that the moon isn't wholly round
but a wafer of fossilized thought.
The Greeks accidentally made it

by imagining that certain
androgynes perched in the sky.
Their collective notion hardened

into this shiny spot installed
in the corners of everyone's eyes.
Science pretends to study it,

astronomers fake up maps.
But everyone knows it's a mote
and nothing like the real moons

orbiting Saturn and Jupiter.
Still, you mustn't eat this relic
as if it were a potato chip.

You're being disrespectful
to ages of faith. Let the pagan
in everyone breathe freely

and enjoy that speck of reflection
affixed where we can find it,
challenging the arrogant dark.

The House of Pale Friendship

Preparing to leave the house
of pale friendship, I choose one
of seven bathrooms in this wing
and polish my teeth, prune my beard,
and scour my hair till it sparks.
When I emerge, I'm immune

to plague that killed the other guests,
rendering them hollow and flimsy.
Packed into coffins, they folded
like rag paper. Their lives left
no residue, no biographies
keening at the ivory moon.

I made no friends among them
except the woman cast in rhinestones
who bounced all night on my bed
while I sat in the only chair
and read a novel by Stephen King.
In the breakfast room everyone

ignored each other except
to gripe about prices and food.
I liked the soggy omelets, burnt
wheat toast, and stale cornflakes,
so I didn't share that small talk.
I can't afford to pay, so plan

to mount a cloud and dissipate.
The landlady reads my poverty
the way I read that eerie novel,
but since I'm the only survivor
offers me a final breakfast.
The house creaks like a downpour.

The glass doors to the patio
bleak with vapor so I step outside
into that vague embrace and feel
the pale friendship for which the house
was famous for a moment or two
while the paying guests were alive.

A Deeper Domestication

Your new refrigerator smiles
in bland stainless complacency.
What's inside? Tomalley, sunchokes,

chortleberries, coils of grape vine.
A quart of starfish milk. A gallon
of the cheapest white wine pressed

from seed pods you found scattered
along Beacon Street last winter
after the snowplows had passed.

So what shall we make for dinner?
Yogurt simmers deep in thought.
A bison steak dreams of the plains.

Because you're a vegetarian
the steak and a bag of chicken wings
will have to rethink themselves.

Maybe a salad: maple and elm
drizzled with a leach of syrup.
Then a brisket of eggplant

roasted in several gay colors
to bring out that challenging flavor
you expect of your favorite meals.

A side dish of sunchokes maybe
garnished with fresh willow twigs
plucked from a Marlborough Street yard.

Your new refrigerator plots
to ensnare us in flavors never
experienced by humans before

digital food was invented
by T-shirts sulking in basements
and longing for California light.

You bought this machine on credit,
and will spend the rest of your life
paying tiny installments drawn

from parts of your body no one,
not even your keenest lovers,
have imagined you possessed.

I touch the stainless shell and feel
the life-force throbbing. Maybe
we should skip dinner and flop

in bed in memory of each other,
our appetites cold and disciplined,
plant-lives learning to relax.

Sea Stars for Sale

Dried for sale, sea stars remind you
that we haven't seen the Atlantic
breathing heavily along a beach
for a couple of plague-struck years.

We could drive to the edge and peer
into the surf and soothe ourselves
with clamburgers from the joint propped
on the lip of the parking lot.

The ocean is a demanding creature.
If we don't visit, it will come
to us with gusty currents shaped
to drag us toward the ultimate depth

where secret phosphorescence prevails.
We live only sixty miles inland
and can't excuse ourselves for missing
appointments with the under-gods.

The sea stars look artificial.
Evolution shaped their poise.
Not all tidepool creatures display
such formal respect. We would,

if we had to live in the shallows.
We would shape exquisite shells
and gladly risk collection
for museums where small children

would gasp covetous little gasps.
Soon the under-gods will die,
and nitrogen runoff will sicken,
and plastic scrap will choke the sea.

If we stand on the beach, we'll catch
a whiff of that prophetic death.
Once the ocean has simplified,
a hurricane will lift and place it

on the altar of entropy,
where we can kneel all creaky
in calcified bodies and offer
the last of our present tense.

A Hole in the World

The fishpond is a hole in the world
through which wanton notions fall.

I often spot couples sparking
in the shadows of the tree line,

their clothing merely a blush.
Sometimes they dance to the lack

of music, unleashing a rhythm
no one has ever conjured before.

I often hear such rhythms but lack
the motive: endearments ripening

in sheaves of unworked metals.
The fish in the fishpond regard

human entanglements with cynical
little eyes. The murder we wreak

in their medium doesn't pass
unnoticed. That's the empowering

thrill of plein air sex—the grasp
of life slipping away with a hook

embedded in its protest. Crimes
of passion are self-punishing

in this pseudo-religious era
when bullying the spirit's a sport.

I want to warn couples that baring
their slippery elements indicts

every landscape they've shared,
mulching toxins from harmless plants

and cracking glacial erratics
that have lounged for thousands of years.

But they won't listen to one man
alone with his personal data.

They're too shy and yet too brazen,
their figurations too postmodern

for the tragic view of life.
Why engage with someone lingering

at water's edge and communing
with brown, brook, and rainbow trout

too large and unsubtle to slip
unnoticed through sunlit shallows?

Water Words

Learning the speech of the river
means listening at night
so sunlight flaking on ripples
doesn't distract from the sifting
of pebbles and silt, or the sigh
of weeds dancing in shallows.

I learned my first words fishing
in the Scantic, brown chords lacing
the fluster of panfish and crawdads.
Later sailing the Connecticut
I heard the whole gravel bottom roar.
An exclamatory island loomed.

Translating insidious tones
into language takes great effort.
Most of my lazy life passed before
I settled on this grassy bank
and put down a taproot to anchor
my carcass in case of flood.

But this is a season of drought,
and the river mumbling to itself
has foregone all its pageantry
and offers a simplified profile.
It hasn't muted, though, its voice
as brassy as a carillon.

I learn the river-words for *angst*
and *fever* and *hungry for fish.*
I also hear a gasp, a whirlpool
that could almost be my name.
No festivals this year, the crimes
against humanity too grave,

too embellished in the sky.
Nothing in nature knows me,
so the river couldn't possibly
enunciate my seven syllables
unless they mean the same thing
as *embrace the flow and drown.*

Some Kind of Retirement Income

Our shabby little beachside
souvenir shop cringes with shame.
The T-shirts, pennants, postcards,
and junk jewelry we offer
would embarrass the coolest huckster.
The hot days ripen like mangoes.

Bikinis flower and fluoresce.
Regardless of race or religion
everyone tans to a painterly
shade of whatever color
they began with. You hide out
in the back room cooking the books,

hoping we can sell this dump
for a profit. I face down
tourists from bristling suburbs
whose children love to shoplift,
who rarely buy without haggling
over the fifty-cent postcards,

which should be three for a dollar,
they claim. Surf at my back all day
graphs on the sand glib arguments
about why the world should end.
We should give up peddling this crap
and open a clam bar. A license

to sell cold beer would solve our debts,
while frying clams, scallops, crab cakes
would relax my old digestive tract
like uncoiling an angry rattler.
Too much work, you say? Maybe
after closing I'll wade in the surf

at dusk, then lie in the sand
where the sun-warm bikinis lay
and let myself evolve enough
to rise into the star-struck distance
with a wingspan broad enough
to cuddle the entire planet.

In Memory of Whitey Bulger

Raking wet leaves into heaps
isn't like harvesting souls
or combing the ocean for pearls.
The air shivers with effort.
The leaves still hostage to trees
rattle in dull old colors
painters abandoned when abstract
expressionism stripped the land.

You rake as hard as I do but
with conviction I can't muster
except as a crude memorial.
The famous gangster I met
decades ago in a Southie bar
has died in prison, his corpse
a mangle of obscene gestures
inflicted by friends of enemies.

I'm raking these leaves in memory
of the beer he bought me, a glass
of Miller's on tap. He murdered
eleven people and subverted
the FBI with his ghostly charm
and surefooted gift of gab.
His small talk was a tombstone
of the purest Carrara marble.
His eyes were flakes of mica
iridescent in the low bar light.

I rake the leaves so pungently
they decay right here at my feet.
You never met him, never saw
half of Boston cringe in his breath,
big men dropping their feral gaze,
women shrinking in the new clothes
they'd bought in Filene's Basement.
The drab October afternoon
falls on its face and whimpers.

You sense the change in the air
but don't realize how the death
of one man perfects a scene
for a moment of abject glory.
I rake and rake, then wheelbarrow
the wrack to compost heaps
at the edge of the woods where
tonight a bear will tumble forth
with playful appetite raving.

A Course in Arson

My summer school course in arson
has gone well. Twelve students
planning their final projects.
I've set only a couple of rules.
They aren't allowed to burn the school,
and can't use gasoline because
it leaves such obvious traces.
Most plan to burn the family home
or business, collect the insurance
to pay their school-year tuition.
The classroom wilts in summer heat.
We discuss the use of wood shavings
or sawdust to start a good hot fire.
We compare beeswax with other,
less expensive candles. Students
argue about the propriety
of using votive candles to spark
crimes that priests in confession
might file among deadly sins.
While we discuss this, fire breaks out
in St Bernard's, just down the street.
The roar of flames is deafening.
The stained glass explodes in colors
more exciting than a car crash.
A flaming nun falls from a tower,
streaking like a banshee. No,
it's only a clot of burning drapery
that puddles smoking on the sidewalk.
Can any student take credit for

this brave sectarian disaster?
No, a drunken priest let a candle
touch his alb. Panicked, he shed it
into a richly upholstered pew
and ran out leaving the big doors
yawning with elegant boredom.
The engines, screaming, arrive
in a glitz of enamel and chrome.
Firefighters attack with hoses
thick as pythons. We return
to the classroom, shivering,
lusty, and thrilled, every student
determined to match fire with fire,
the orange glare caught in their gaze
and the smell of ash on their breath.

Lizzie Borden Day

"In the spirit if not the mode
of the Renaissance emblem poem,
Marvell's garden poems deploy
the notion of *green* to invoke
the innocence of our founding myth
and the modern sense of renewal."

Such was the thesis I failed
to etch into the stone tablets
I lugged to a professor's lair
on the third flood of a revamped
townhouse on the BU campus.
My lack of clarity appalled

like thunder at dawn. Renewing
that shame, I rise into gloom
of secular rain, a storm brewing
in full glory a few miles south.
My garden, unlike Marvell's,
lacks the innocence of dogma,

and flaunts its green libido
more aggressively than survival
requires. Today, Lizzie Borden Day,
the groan of logging machinery,
a herd of giant chippers,
competes with actual thunder

to compost as much of the planet
as its collective maw can swallow.
Marvell would rise in Parliament,
the angry member from Hull,
and protest this wanton ravishment.
I cower at my desk and propose

a thesis thirty years too late.
The rain and thunder drift east,
the sky mellows in tepid grays,
and Lizzie Borden, fresh from her grave,
waves her hatchet to warn me
that running amok won't do.

East of Quabbin, North of Ware

Lost in mid-Massachusetts
east of Quabbin, north of Ware,
we feel the roads unravel

like cheap clothes, revealing landscapes
rimmed with hickory and poplar,
fired by a globule of moon.

Route thirty-two splits and meanders
through towns where only neon
pizza signs spark any color

to challenge the dominate gray.
Even a golf course looks haunted,
trembling like a drumhead. We talk

to keep our spirits up. My father,
shrouded by an oxygen tent
in the intensive care unit,

infected us with fear of death.
The moon engraves its faith on our faces
as we watch the unmapped landscape

heave and toss and give up houses
the way the sea gives up shells.
That people live here's no comfort.

What do they do when courage fails
and the night becomes too personal?
Our headlights plunge bravely forward

but can’t plumb the living heart
of matter, never mind the dark
that upholsters the quaking ego.

Tree Aflame on a Power Line

A tree aflame on a power line
brightens the hurricane sky.
We dodge under it as quickly
as we dare. Acetylene-bright,
the glare ornaments the drab
and rumpled sky with a festive
defiance of the heavy rain.
You've never seen this violet hue
before, but I remember it
flashing in the midnight hills
when as a child I lay awake
convinced that the stars themselves
were landing to dispense their favors
among the chosen few, like me.
I don't know whether huge gouts
of foxfire or fragments of dream
illuminated those distant slopes.
But precisely this shade of violet
flared and in a few moments died,
leaving an afterimage dark
as the imagined light had been bright.
This bonfire of tree and power pole
is actual enough to deprive us
of electricity and phone line
for several hours to come. Yet
watching it burn exhilarates
with primal notions arsonists
and firefighters share. You insist
on driving home and leaving

the fire for firefighters to enjoy;
but I'm so dark with childhood
that the impossible violet flame
burns sixty years of adulthood
away, leaving nothing but nature
elemental enough to blame.

Two Dead in Local House Fire

Roaring and threatening collapse,
the house at North and Taylor
burned on a windy autumn night
and smelted a youngish couple,
leaving love letters for us
firefighters to mull over
back at the station at dawn.

I drove past the weedy vacancy
last year. No stick of house remains
after half a century of ghosts.
The lot borders and blends into
thirty acres of potato field.
No one will build on that grave
with its tangle of maple saplings.

Considering the ripe black soil,
the farmer should plow right through
the lingering miasma and plant
potatoes to exorcise the weeds
and let the dead couple regress
properly in time and space,
their naked forms dispersing.

I was seventeen when I climbed
from the ladder into the wreck
of their charred bedroom and stepped
carefully over the bodies
toasted mellow by fatal smoke.

I wielded a heavy brass nozzle
to snuff tatters of lingering fire.

Sometimes the victims return
not in sleep or dream but strolling
in billows of creamy sunlight.
I hope they've written a few more
love letters and forgotten the fire,
which after these many tepid years
has surely forgotten them.

The Pneumatic Zoo of Synthesis

At the pneumatic zoo of synthesis, animals explode into other animals. Sometimes they exchange themselves one-to-one. Sometimes they form whole families, swarms, or even herds. A family of mice becomes a single garter snake. A woodchuck becomes a pangolin. An elephant becomes a herd of Jersey cows. You ask how it works. A machine creates a powerful vacuum. The animal enters and is both collapsed and expanded. It steps back into normal pressure in whatever form it wishes. A horse becomes a dragon. A chimera becomes a family of skunks. A zebra slips out of its stripes and becomes a camel. You wonder if it would work with humans. We know it does: that fat pink male attorney used to be a postcard bathing beauty. An old woman became a set of newborn twins. But beware. Our former President stepped into the vacuum and exploded into an army of cockroaches. Now they're busy chewing on Brooklyn. So don't attempt it, although we could enter together and perhaps emerge as a unicorn, ready for a prince to ride.

A Cloud Mountain

The dusk above Epping bulks
with black cloud on blue-black sky.
The blur of oncoming headlights
ribbons in a tough endless glitter.

We're driving west toward Manchester
but appear about to drill a hole
in a nameless, unmapped mountain.
The oncoming cars have escaped

a crushing and desolate fate
toward which our lane of taillights
rushes without hesitation.
We're too overwrought to parse

the illusion of a huge mountain
that dissolves as dark overflows
and swallows the sky's geometries.
You focus so firmly on driving

that I must keep us both awake
with unnatural chatter about
the numbing flatness of southeast
New Hampshire, the over-lit

gas stations and convenience stores
crouched beside every off-ramp.
Driving headlong into the night
we're so engorged with traffic

that our bodies tense with the pain
of an accident that won't occur
but still lurks around every bend
with its blue and red lights flashing.

Living on the Borderland

Keats thrived in liminal landscapes
north of London. Meadow faced
suburban villa. Marshland fumed
and the high road jangled. The boy
poet nuzzled the threatened world
of badger, hedgehog, newt and frog
and sang in his favorite colors
against the sin of enclosure.

In my own childhood I focused
on the borders of things. A rock
held up against the sky. Where
does rock end and sky begin?
Myopic, I felt along the frame
that encloses everything, the line
between turtle shell and water,
between self and vacant space.

When I held that rock why weren't
child and rock a single being?
Like but unlike Keats I stepped
forward and committed myself
to fondling the edges of things,
where sea horizons blur in mist
and city streets acned with potholes
reveal earth-scape hidden below.

The genius of Keats seized myth
translated into psychic gestures

larger than life. Titans brooding
in massive bowers no human
would dare attempt to inhabit.
I settled for algae green ponds
and the ruins of old brick mills,
hardly challenging the limits.

The silence I met at Keats' grave
under that pyramid in Rome
lingers like a frog in my throat.
Three times his age at his death
I can't speak one word in pastels
as delicate as his, the raw earth
refusing to distinguish itself
from his glad expenditure of flesh.

The Visionary Company

Following bear tracks at dusk
I'm less than a mile from home
but the forest cramps like a muscle
and mist smokes from the dirty snow
and conceals me from myself.

I turn to retrace my boot prints
but they've disappeared. Figures
congeal in the watery gloom—
husky as Blake illustrations
but with muddled expressions.

The figures crumple as the mist
thickens and the light fades. Of course
they weren't really Los or Urizen
or other psychic malfunctions
but gauzy shadows woven

by the solstice to warn me
to get home before dark. I tromp
east and smell wood smoke curdling
from a metal stack. Emerging
from the woods, I observe my boot prints

sidling to the edge of the yard,
then returning. Have I stayed home
after all? I creep to the house,
peer in a window. There I am,
watching a football game, Patriots

versus the Jets, blue shirts and green.
I look so comfortable with teacup
and book in my lap. Returning
to the forest, I retrace the tracks
I didn't make but must be there.

If I look hard enough maybe
those shadows will become figures
again, and the crowd of us
will track the bear to its den
and cuddle up with it. Then winter

with a renewed sense of purpose
will expend itself in storms as drab
as the shades of gray we members
of the visionary company
wear for glory, not for warmth.

River Lore

Because I fall into the river
almost daily you assume
I want to become a merman
and marry a fish. This autumn
the river runs high and cold.

The houses that overlook it
clutch the earth in fear of flood.
At the edge of the parking lot
where I usually fall in
children are teasing each other

while their mothers complain
about their greasy husbands
reeking of stale beer and butts.
If I married a fish I'd live
in a universal solvent

and always smell fresh enough
to dine with A-list celebrities.
Do you think that's what I want?
I fall into the river because
you push me, then back away,

hoping I'll drown soundlessly.
The river laps at its banks
with eager pubescent kisses.
It samples everything and laves
a sickly love on the landscape.

When I fall in, I slip under
so deeply I touch the living,
evolving flesh of the planet.
You don't understand that rivers
are wounds that don't want to heal.

You don't realize that mermaids
and mermen consort with fish
because desperate to embrace
a medium in which human
hunger no longer prevails.

Photoshopped

That snapshot of me talking
with T. S. Eliot is fake.
Also, that photo of me combing
Ezra Pound's overwrought beard.
Also, the one of me lighting
Wallace Stevens' bullish cigar.

Whoever forged these pictures
has a gnarly sense of humor.
Selling them as postcards is fraud.
Did you make them? Did you tuck
them in the bookshop knowing
they would publicly embarrass me?

You photoshopped these images
to illuminate the autumn dark
and render my life's work foolish.
Why didn't you depict me
attending to Marianne Moore
or rescuing Sylvia Plath

from her gas oven's grisly maw?
The owner of the bookshop admits
he found the photos unlikely,
but displayed them by the register.
He has sold nearly all. I go limp
in the café and try to drown
in coffee the color of rawhide.

You will never apologize.
but pay for the coffee with a laugh.
Throw in a couple of scones,
the kind all famous old men
eat with their dentures clacking.

SX-70 Redux

Polaroid photos discolor
with age, their complex emulsions
yellowing and shedding faces
of people who have since aged or died.
Those rootless faces go adrift
and snag in the autumn forest.

I see them shake in the breeze
and regret having photographed
their original flesh-framed selves.
One or two of those snapshots
display my own sour face
with its unwieldy gray expression.

Some feature your famous sneer.
A couple time-warp my father,
caught trimming a Christmas tree
forty years ago, when winter
still expressed itself in snowstorms
whose purity is no longer likely.

I could thrust my aluminum
ladder into the woods and rescue
a few of these ghostly faces,
but they're only bits of vapor.
Chemicals decayed over years
and changed into other chemicals,

that no one has thought to study.
You don't want me to bother
with these past-tense people,
even if some of them are us.
You want me to stop staring
up into the trees and return

to the hopeless task of raking
leaves from the gravel driveway.
Let those muddled faces drift off
wherever our exhausted souls go,
and let's tire our present tense
with honest, if useless, labor.

On the Subway Station Floor

Slumped on the subway station floor
I chew on my plaid wool jacket,
gnawing a cuff while the famous
Chinese poet with both small hands
sketches a famous landscape
in the greasy underground air.

Passersby throw coins at us
because we look too deviant
to survive on our wits. Trains growl
from the tunnels and open their doors
but the moment hasn't arrived.
The Chinese poet regards me

chewing my sleeve and requests
my genealogy. I reply
through a muffling of wool that
the tank-rumpled Ukraine mud
swallowed half my ancestors
while the others lie preserved

in the bogs of Ireland. He nods
and begins a new sketch. No need
to ask if his great-great grandfather
was that same calligrapher
whose work in the Boston museum
sobered me one rainy afternoon

while the guards snoozed on their feet
and mammoth carved Buddhas mused.
No need to translate the scroll
embellished with a reedy pond
set in a hillscape overhung
by black vees of birds. The trains

roar like revenge. The coins fall
about us, nickels and quarters
not like teardrops but more like
bullet holes punched in the concrete.
I've chewed my jacket long enough
and my friend has finished his sketch

so we gather the coins and leap
aboard a train. As it leaves
the station, I note our ghosts
still reposing where we left them,
their smiles as fixed as graffiti,
their perfection simple as stone.

Evil Ballerina Naked in Snowstorm

The evil ballerina poses
naked in a snowstorm. Her skin
is the rind of a melon except
where the seams pucker. Photos
will prove she was manufactured,
not born. Wielding your camera,
you feel great crosscurrents flow
from one art form to another.

At last she dances, defying wind
from the northeast. You snap photo
after photo, but the snow blurs
the features for which the public
will pay real money, while the cold
by rippling and combing trees
whispers of intimate moments
ordinary people rarely share.

The evil ballerina prances
amid the drifts. She leaves tracks
dainty as deer-prints. Her body's pale
as the storm, and for a moment
you wonder if she's really there.
But she explodes on tiptoe, flaunting
her neutral expression to spite
desires only masochists indulge.

You wrap a blanket around her
and guide her toward the warm indoors

to confide woman to woman.
But she breaks away and twirls
into the slanting storm, leaping
and kicking like a runaway colt
and leaving you with camera slung
around your neck and the shame
of remaining discreetly clothed.

An Existential Symptom

A persistent dry cough dredges
the mud and muck collected
in the bilge of my lung-sacks,

exposing discarded objects
at the bottom of my being.
Nothing to do with Jean-Paul

Sartre, Heidegger, or Camus,
heroes and villains of youth.
Something to do with Nanette,

the sleekest young woman in town,
who tried to pierce my shyness
and failed, retreating to her house

on Sword Avenue, a dead-end
down by the double-track railroad.
I wonder if after fifty years

she remembers my auburn gaze,
fixed yet frightened. I wonder
if the railroad, reduced to one track,

retains a trace of youthful spoor.
The cough bothers me, maybe the virus
toppling half a million a day.

Maybe I should phone my doctor
and cough in his one good ear.
Maybe I should drive a hundred

miles to Sword Avenue and swoon
in front of Nanette's former home.
Easier to reread the ancient

existentialists and pretend
that my high school reading still applies.
Coughing through the year end dark,

I dredge up from my innards
bits of obsolete machinery,
clots of mildewed paper, scruff

of the clothes I sported in youth.
What would the medical world
make of my brand of plague?

The sun won't rise today. The cough
erupts like a rude observation,
corrugating every verb and noun.

Epistle to Bob Dylan

Stuck inside the bluest eye. Glass shatters, but the cops won't respond. The railroad shivers like a zipper unzipped in a parked car. How can anyone be so desperate? A freight train stumbles along, every second car derailing. I want to stop this unraveling, but despite the lack of law enforcement I'm under arrest. Who has witnessed my crimes? Who has signed a statement literate enough to convict me? The bluest eye winks. Who stands behind that weary flirtation? Who has the courage to blame me for her favorite sins? The end nears. It bears the snout of a '49 Chrysler. No rust, only a sheen of paste wax tough as exegesis.

Let's do everything twice. Two blue eyes, each bluer than the other. A double-tracked railroad with competing trains travelling in both directions at once. The cops agree to release me to oversee my reincarnation as the famous painter who died in Tahiti more than a century ago. Flat planes of color. Naked people sprawled on the beach as the tsunami approaches. Maybe I'll run for office. Maybe I'll volunteer to serve on the Nobel Prize committee, where I'll vote only for creation science, voodoo economics, and literature shaped like zeppelins. No one will contradict me, but the stink of gin will soil the process, confirming that the bluest eye went blind in childhood, leaving a whisper of ash.

Dismantling the Penitent

God told him to do it. The hand
severed and tossed in a basket,
he'd paraded the stump down Main Street.

Hours passed. On all fours in
the cosmos, he watched the surgeons
struggle to reattach the hand.

He considered their effort wasted
since he didn't need those hands: claws
of a lobster: feet a pair of clams.

God had told him the desert drank
more blood than he could drink beer.
In heavy breath, stars blew past

with silvery balloon shapes dulling.
God told him the razor sketched fire:
it felt like fire. The doctors clenched

fistfuls of sutures. A calling,
he thought, a calling was all
these meat-conservators needed

to choke their gossip and trip them
frankly to their knees. The hand leapt
from the surgical grasp to float

unlamented through the ceiling
and join the child who'd abandoned it
lifetimes ago, long before his birth.

Roughhewn Summer Afternoon

People lean into the wind,
their summer clothes fluttering,
expressions deeply clarified.
I'm almost proud of our species.

The avenue points straight to the sea,
from which all blessings flow.
The skyscrapers lean like the people,
but with stiff aesthetic dignity

rather than loose-limbed humor.
I haven't lived in the city for years,
but feel its opulence crystallize
in glitter of filtered sunlight,

plate glass brimming and brick
absorbing every taint of gloom.
The crowd surges toward the harbor
where restaurants feature the fish

that will soon be extinct. Oysters
imported from the south pose
on ice, their thoughts unknowable.
Lobsters conspire in big square tanks.

I'm talking myself into lunch,
but it's a long walk to the pier
where my favorite scallops broil.
Watching the wind off the water

angle people into postures
comic as old silent movies,
I realize that we're regressing
with gestures that define like runes.

Only the finest of seductions,
rare events, can shape us to fit
each other, leaving no residue
weeping in the corners of the park.

Symbols, Emblems, Metaphors

Someone stretched a clothesline
across a woods road and hung
a new blue flannel-lined shirt
and a placard with the number
40 printed neatly on it.

I think I can wear the shirt
without catching some disease,
but the number worries me.
Forty acres and a mule?
Unbuilt house number 40

in some evil future subdivision?
Forty years subtracted from
the life of anyone who dares
to don this L. L. Bean shirt
that looks, feels, and smells unworn?

No one else ever walks this road,
which ends in a marsh where birds
never sing. Winter is closing in
with tepid gusts. I'll wear this shirt
home, and nail up the plaque where

anyone might see it and wonder.
Symbols, emblems, metaphors
incite the challenge of dullards
like me who believe in reason
and distinguish verbs from nouns.

I already own a shirt like this,
but a paler shade of blue. I passed
the age of forty almost forty
years ago. What else can happen?
As I turn toward home wearing

the shirt and clutching the number,
I feel the wind become a language
all over again, just because
I'm facing the other direction,
as if turning back the clock.

Red Lilies: A Still-Life

Red lilies in a vase declare
themselves with painful voices.

The table on which they squat
looks as shaky as something painted

by Matisse in his foulest moods.
But you aren't a painted figure.

With prim mockery you feign
a pose that lacks poise, a shy

creature concealing rugged claws.
Last night Beth the cat hooked my thumb

in play. The pain was exquisite,
threading up my arm to settle

in the forecourt of my brain.
As I washed the wound a picture

of red lilies on a table formed
that by the next day, today,

had completed itself with you.
Christmas day, cold enough for good

King Wenceslaus to do his deed.
The snow slouches like a huddle

of delinquents. The light arises
with reluctance. You remain

seated by the table of lilies
although their outrageous red

puzzles you. How did I dream up
such palpable flowers and place

their vulgarity on a table
that wasn't here a day ago?

You as well as I project
a still life we saw in a book.

If you rise from your chair, you'll shatter
the illusion, and the red lilies

will scatter like embers fresh
from the stove, good for melting ice.

A Live Grenade

Plodding through a prescribed text
at dawn, you handle your bible
like a live grenade. The shimmer
of angelic choirs rarely bathes you
in the trills for which you long.
The naked face of deity
neither endorses or reproaches
your little bookish ritual.
But sometimes when we're crossing
a raving boulevard you glow
a moment with unearthly passion—
a flavor you never share in public
or private but have hoarded
for the last, fatal implosion
when all your resources combine
with subatomic fervor.
Thus the live grenade. I wonder
when you'll pull the pin. Our friend
died on Monday, leaving his books
to Goodwill, his tired old clothes
to the tired old poor of Brighton,
his tired old spouse to herself.
The stroke that killed him still lurks
in the darkest room of his house.
We should think of him instead
of the frugal breakfast we'll share
when you tire of courting spirits
of mainly historical interest.
You'd never attempt to invoke

the dead of our lives; but sometimes
when you trot off for a morning
of napping at the Athenaeum
you leave a wake the color of stars.
Maybe Dutch-Reformed Melville
would hear a hymn in your footfall.
But all I hear is the snicker
of your animus pulling the pin
from that metaphorical grenade,
threatening to blast away
all four dimensions, disproving
the laws of physics that keep us
from toppling into ourselves.

Road Trip

Snouted and ugly as a coffin,
Sunkist orange and wedge-shaped,
my new car meets the highway
at so steep an angle I plow
a ditch three feet deep, splaying
chunks of asphalt and forcing
oncoming traffic off the road.
The state police smile as I pass.
The highway crews wave. Driving south,
I ditch the interstate through Hartford,
New Haven, Bridgeport, Norwalk,
and finally hit Manhattan.

Trenching Fifth Avenue I unearth
gas and electric lines, sewage
and water pipes, ripping the fabric
to expose the plumbing no one
wants to see. Crossing subway lines,
I scrape the concrete tunnels raw,
and farther south reveal the bones
of the old city: brick foundations,
slate gravestones, pewter pots, bottles,
and mildewed bibles stinking
of grief that should've resolved
itself two centuries ago.

Pedestrians laugh and applaud.
Few have seen this sort of car
before, but soon everyone

will have one. On I drive,
scorching through Washington Square,
toppling the chessboards and addicts,
harrowing the financial district
then drilling through Battery Park,
crashing and sinking the Staten
Island ferry and pointing
my prow at Ellis Island,
where my ancestors first ran aground.

On a Beach in the Carolinas

The deadweight of tropical storms
almost smothers the ocean.
Although winds avenge themselves
in gloomy colors, the effect
doesn't impress anyone

but boaters risking their bones.
I've often found myself washed up
on a beach in the Carolinas
where crab shells crackle and strops
of seaweed drape pebbles at tideline.

The aftermath erases recall
of the storm. A few houses tilt
the wrong way. A parking lot
features knee-deep drifts of sand.
It's always like this: solitude

and reluctance to apologize
for vicissitudes of climate change.
I don't know why the Carolinas
instead of Cape Cod or Nantucket,
more familiar, closer to home.

Why do I find myself leering
into the carcass of a shark,
its liver eaten by an orca?
Only along the warmer beaches
do such horrors stir the soul.

I prop myself on my elbows
and look past the dead fish
out to sea where spume and mist
blend in those luscious pastels
I've coveted all my life.

To embrace such a stippled horizon
has always been my ambition.
But the storms of summer preclude
the meditative calm required
to trace the curve of the planet.

Wrack of beach glass, plastic shards,
pulp and stone and rotting flesh
frame me in a self-portrait
that vicious weather will someday
hang on the slope of the heavens.

Abandoned Supermarket

The abandoned supermarket reeks
of famine. The last shoppers
left snail trails in aisles that warped
when rain breeched the big flat roof.

I'm searching for useable scrap,
hoping to scrounge enough lumber
to build a woodshed to shelter
a couple of cords for winter.

The long empty shelves rebuke
like eyebrows lifted in disdain.
Nothing left even for mice to eat.
The bankruptcy shocked everyone,

including the manager, who locked
himself in his office and wept
while his workforce looted the last
cartloads of summer produce.

Another year and the roof
will collapse, but the concrete walls
will outlast the ruins of Rome,
unless someone bulldozes them.

I disassemble plywood gondolas
and load them in my pickup.
Police cruise past but assume,
because I'm working in daylight,

I've been hired to salvage scrap.
Others have preceded me, stealing
metal fixtures and copper wire.
Someone stripped all the plumbing,

leaving the rest rooms gaping
like gawkers at a fatal crash.
No other supermarket for miles.
Most of us can't afford food

anymore, and live off the land.
Come winter, we'll bloat and burst
and armed vigilantes will arrive
to relieve us of our possessions.

Black-robed justice will prevail,
but the stink of mold and dead mice
will thicken in the coldest months,
leaving nothing useful to say.

Dead on Time

One of those snotty old TV dramas only I rewatch. The inspector is in love with the widow. She's not merry. She plans suicide to reunite herself with her husband. He killed himself with her help. Because he suffered from some unnamed palsy his finger couldn't find the trigger. Sure to be fatal. Being a professor, like me, he had decided to take the dignified way out. Not me. I want to go screaming, kicking, and cursing into the seamless dark. The professor and his wife made love forever, then stopped. That's when suicide loomed. The disease was just an excuse. The inspector tries to control the situation, but the widow offs herself anyway. The fury of the inspector is boundless. He riots in the police station and sets on pikes the heads of his sergeant and superintendent. A couple of constables, too. Meanwhile the dead woman is walking again. She only pretended to be dead on time. When she reaches the station and sees the heads on pikes, she fails to realize that these are her cloudy trophies hung in the sky. The inspector emerges. He doesn't recognize her. On his way to the nearest pub he mutters, "I wonder who that woman was? Well, none of my business." So it ends. I may have gotten a few details wrong, but the credits are rolling and it's too late to change anything.

Trivia from the Otherworld

Ghosts of lost or broken objects
trouble us. Keys, can openers,
hi-fi equipment, power drills,
plumbing parts, TVs, toys
from best forgotten childhoods,
pocketknives, cook pots, screwdrivers,
cars that died on the highway.

These linger, haunting the low ground
of our bank accounts, trilling
like peepers in bloodstained dawn.
Sometimes they brush against us
in memory of better times.
Sometimes we spot them sulking
in the corners of our vision.

Others have written about loss
and rendered it graceful. Days
of wine and goat cheese picnics, nights
with friends who died in their sleep.
Elegies of tender regard draped
in colors worn by royalty
when breeding wasn't just for dogs.

We're too petty for such curlicues
of sentiment. My favorite hammer,
my model trains, my green sweater.
Your yellow blouse, your shoes that fit,
your Kitchen Aid mixer, the gloves

you wore on that cold night walking
from the hotel to the opera house.

Our landscapes are haunted by refuse.
Don't you think it's time to exorcise
the nether regions of our lives?
We must clean up after ourselves
and learn to forget those objects
whose mundane spirits promise
no comfort after we're dead.

Epistle to Anne Carson

Open boat in this weather? Old gym socks drape the pines. Melodies shaped like telephone conversations bubble over. Out here on the lake, the chop the color of sardines, we observe each other so closely our eyes touch and threaten to adhere. As we turn away to face opposite shores, a clap of one hand pretends to be thunder. We aren't fooled. The crisis will come later, when we row to Noel's pier in hopes of a cocktail party with the neighbors apologizing for voting for the wrong ticket. The dogs will refrain from barking but will give us that look. You know the one: glass-eyed but crazy with intelligence. If people blush at birth and death, what does that say about the residue adrift in the great between? As you row I drag a hand in the water. It's so cold it fondles like a greeting from the grave. Someone called the sea a grave. Marianne Moore, of course. But this modest lake poured between two wooded ridge lines lacks the epic grandeur to which the sea always aspires and usually achieves. If you row harder and faster we'll dock right at sunset, insofar as the gabardine sky allows us to imagine it. Already I can taste my gin and tonic, colder even than the lake, and deeper, much deeper, with strangers like us drowned in the depths.

An Iridescent Mood

In an iridescent mood I cross
the frozen marsh to explore
the forest beyond. Skunks and fox
scatter, but the purple brown
tree trunks remain aloof. Years ago
I tracked myself through these woods
and found blood spoor in the snow.
Since then I've dreamed of bones gnawed
in the leaf-fall, gutted carcasses
abandoned by hunters, stone-lined
cellar holes gradually healing.

Today I'm scouting for nests perched
in leafless boughs to determine
if we're losing all our songbirds
or if they've retreated deeper
into lonely woods to evade us
and our storms of microplastics.
I count a few nests but not enough
to account for last spring's lack of song
in my neighborhood. No thrush
or painted grosbeak, hardly a sparrow
or phoebe. Winter looms ahead,
the forest upholstering in drifts
heavy enough to keep me indoors.
Ten days before Christmas, though,
only a dusting of snow preserves
my footfall for whomever follows.

When I circle back to the marsh
I feel that follower closing in
so I lengthen my stride and cross
the ice-slick in two or three minutes
and reach the paved road where friendly
dog-walkers brighten the landscape.
When my shadow catches up with me
I re-incorporate it into myself
and go home still iridescent
enough to light the pages
of some harmlessly readable book.

On the Edge of Technology

Living on the edge of technology suits me. Only slightly wired in, I spark easily, drawing as little current as possible. You claim to be battery powered, but I detect a trail of sixteen-gauge wire leading somewhere. Oh, it stretches to the coffee shop. Regulars rehearse their digital careers on laptops while slurping coffee dispensed by women sporting aggressive but slightly misshapen bosoms. The men who dish the deli food are a little awry, too, angled to the south. Your tail of wire leads me to the long counter where the loneliest freelancers sniffle over apps they've designed but can't get to work. "Let me try," I tell one bearded young fellow. He casts a downcast while I fiddle with his code. A spark leaps from my left or negative paw to his right or positive paw. The app flames into being. Within a few seconds it has earned half a billion dollars in ad revenue. He thanks me by paying for my coffee. I'm touched. You've observed this male bonding from a safe distance. Now you coil up your wires and scuttle to the parking lot, weeping with either shame or joy.

Windchill Fifty Below

Blame the weather on Karl Marx
and his fey historical outlook.
Blame it on Nietzsche and his grim
supermen posing for sculptors.

Blame it on Hoover for naming
himself after a famous dam.
Just don't blame me for stoking
a wood fire that makes us sneeze

while shattering the ingrown cold.
We don't dare step outside where
the smoke of different fossil fuels
mingles with burning oak and ash

to compose a ghost we admire
for showing itself in daylight.
Where can we go to escape
the arctic air that stifles

conversations we don't enjoy
with people whose names we forget?
The new owner of the bookshop
expects us to buy a book.

The barista expects us to drink
his bravest and boldest espresso.
The checkout clerk who fondles
our groceries expects an exchange

of wishes for a lovely day.
It isn't lovely, Wind chills down
to fifty below zero. Engines
refuse to turn over. Batteries

of electric vehicles withdraw
their favors. Let's stay home and read
until we erupt like children,
the doubtful parts of us keening.

Kumimanu at Large

We learn that giant penguins
roamed the seas after dinosaurs
petered out. Kumimanu, twice
the height, three times the bulk
of the emperor penguin,
would have savaged the fish-world
almost as cruelly as humans have.

You peer at the skeletal drawing
and realize that many neighbors
and friends we encounter downtown
are giant penguins adapted to life
on land, appetites adjusted
to include coffee, bagels, pizza.

You note that the beak and stance
expose them. Pronged conversations
and short legs clever on ice
distinguish them from those born
fully human and incapable
of enjoying long stretches at sea.

Many will see this article
about fossils in New Zealand
and surely some will notice
that their beaked friends and neighbors
never reveal their torsos because
their feathers would give them away.

They must be cozy in winter,
but summer would be a challenge.
We wonder if they're susceptible
to bird flu. Maybe their doctors,
alert to their genetic heritage,
vaccinate them so thoroughly
they can't endanger the village.

Let's hope so. Don't mention
this article to friends who
seem to be giant penguins.
They've impersonated persons
all their lives, so leave them
to foster their eggs in peace.

Malicious Mischief

The red house on the corner has digested its inhabitants. Police arrive with putty knives and scrapers, but they can't collect much residue. The evidence points to me. I incited this house to turn against its owners. No, I deny everything. I had merely commented that an early nineteenth-century house with barn-red shingles looks independent and probably doesn't need anyone looking after it. But that was silly: houses need to be inhabited. The red house glares at me. I've made trouble for it. But the police can't charge a house with a crime, so they charge me with malicious mischief. I immediately confess: I've always wanted to be guilty of malicious mischief. It's like running amok, which I've always wanted to do, although not sure how to do it. The police will explain when I get to the station. After I've passed out all the bribes, they'll give me a copy of *The Mischief Maker's Manual*, and in the future, I'll live by it.

Something Ugly

Something ugly about this dinner. Maybe the fish-face staring up at me. Maybe the deep-fat-fried bull testicles. Maybe the stinging nettle salad. Maybe the hog's blood wine. I lean into my food with what I hope is an enthusiastic smirk. I don't know the people who invited me to dinner. They look rich, but serving live ants, big red ones, for hors d'oeuvres didn't win my friendship. I suppose they mean well but discussing over food the war crimes their grandfather committed in the Second World War doesn't win me over, either. Not that they care. I think they invited me because they saw my photo in the paper and thought I must be a local celebrity, since the article was neither a wedding announcement nor an obituary. Although I didn't see the paper, I assume it was reporting my arrest for throwing a pie at our First Selectman at town meeting. I missed him but caught the Second Selectman square in the kisser. The police chief laughed and laughed until I nailed him with a pie, too. Now I'm out on bail and we're having pie for dessert. With a hoot and holler my hosts fling pies at each other and at me. I duck, but the third or fourth thrown pie smacks me full-face and at last I realize why they invited me: for my sense of play. I grab a couple of pies and soon we're all dripping cream and custard, normal food at last.

Otherworldly

Alien spacecraft spangle the dusk. I often see them hovering in the corners of my eyes. This evening there are more than usual. Maybe this is an invasion. Usually it's an evasion, which is why many refuse to believe that anyone would fly from the other side of the galaxy to peer at our little civilization. But then I don't know where they come from. Maybe as nearby as the dark side of the moon. Although its lack of atmosphere suggests otherwise. Sometimes the aliens deplane in my back yard and poke around my garden like oversized rabbits. Since I don't grow vegetables, they nibble daylilies and phlox, Maybe flowers are their preferred diet. I don't mind their little depredations, and the scorch marks left by their craft don't offend me. I just hope they don't accidentally spark a fire. Some dark night when I hear them muttering in the foliage I'll step outside with a camera and catch them in the act. Then everyone will have to believe. Of course other people see them, too, but many mistake them for members of competing but earthly political parties. I know better. They're too polite, and their appetite for flowers doesn't chime with the lust for power that engages our ruling class.

Winter Weasel Afoot

A white bolt across the yard,
into the barn, around the barn,
into the coop, out with a mouse.

The weasel's faster than snow,
subtler than a farewell kiss,
bolder than a stroke of luck.

Already the day pardons itself,
tearing at its clothes, weeping.
That slain mouse emits a ghost

in exquisite gray tones people
like us envy. You note that
the weasel's winter outfit

is fluff as bright as a deer's.
I respect its appetite, honed
by cunning no human can match.

The weasel didn't rouse the hens
but savaged the mouse and ran
to a lair we haven't discovered.

You want to reinforce the coop,
fence it with warnings and threats,
but the weasel will find its way.

We've only three hens. Stash them
in the basement every night
until weasel season ends.

The days telescope and fade
so quickly they hardly seem real.
Christmas overstates itself

as usual, parking a blushing rump
on the village green and sighing
for the lost vicissitudes of youth.

The weasel punctures and punctuates
the solstice with tracks we could trace
across the frozen yellow marsh

to some ulterior landscape
where standard dogmas don't apply
and hunger always feels welcome.

A Poet Becomes a Bluebell

She argues with her roots, but they hold as firmly as sea anchors. She argues with her blossoms, but they tenderize her worst impulses, and she cries into the rain. Her husband herds the children into the house for dinner and baths and bedtime stories about people turning into flowers and flowers turning into people. Because their mother is a famous poet and occupies all of England, Scotland, and Wales, they must never know that she has become a bluebell. It would discourage them from attending university. Even if their mother reverts to human form her stem looks unsteady, and she might not be able to read her bluebell poem at King William's coronation. But in her poem, in all her poems, she's both subject and object. She's also a verb. What happened to her stringy colorless hair? Who is now wearing the lace collar she saves for special occasions? Becoming a bluebell is not a special occasion. Nor is the coronation of King William. What's special is rooting in her favorite spot in the garden and defying her husband to contradict her. Business as usual, the rich loam fraught with earthworms.

A Bluebell Becomes a Poet

Its lanky root system gels into thighs and calves. Its treasured shade of blue gives way to flimsy translucent human hair. It tries to clench its blossom to avoid embarrassing itself, but soon it's bleating in vowels and consonants. It has a husband, a soft-looking fellow who looks after the kids but won't help with the garden. The bluebell feels compelled to compose a poem about a bluebell becoming a poet. But isn't that premature? The flower has yet to figure out how to operate a mobile creature, how arms and legs avoid tangling with each other, how the digestive system works. After fuddling around for a while the former bluebell sets to work. She realizes that she's female and therefore fraught with responsibilities. She must reassure her children. She must comfort her husband. She must finish her poem for King William's coronation. She tries to think like a person, but flower knowledge boils over. The root-feel of soil, the moisture ascending into stem and leaf., the ripple of petals in a breeze. *Replace it all with sex*, she writes. She writes but hasn't yet learned to read. No matter. Sound out the muddle and let someone else edit it. Some other species. This one's too clumsy and raw.

Lampman

The horror we call Lampman
prowls along a gravel road
where last spring's anemones failed.

Forest crowds the dark. Houses
spaced a quarter mile apart
close as tightly as oysters

against his gray phosphorescence.
We're not certain that he's dead
but his fitful glow suggests

at least the notion of decay.
He walks this road every night
and no one challenges him.

As we pass in our car we imagine
he waves, but his glow occludes
his vestigial form and gestures.

He isn't much. Hardly a presence.
But we mustn't stop to talk.
We might become pillars of salt

the rain would erode and erase.
Lampman creeps from point to point,
never returning along this road.

Where does he go in daylight?
Is he present but unseen because
his glow is too vague to compete

with the honest November sun?
People blame him for the deaths
that frequent the nearby houses,

but cancer and old age apply.
No murders, no violent accidents,
no screams from vacant bedrooms,

no skulls grinning after midnight.
Lampman shuffles along the road
in his self-sparked illumination,

an idea of a person rather
than a soul on its own. When
we see him, we feel depleted

although he has never troubled us
except by exposing to starlight
a dream life we'd rather hide.

Opening the Season

The fluster of December snow
enlightens without comforting.
Up before light, I gulp a mouthful
of indoor angst to sustain me,
then step into boots and regress
to my childhood of snowmen and ice.

The evergreens aren't discouraged
by the trimmings on their boughs.
Only a couple of inches.
No need to rouse the snow blower
from its den, its fiery breath
medieval enough to kill me
if I'm careless in handling it.

Maybe behind the shuck of cloud
dawn's rosy fingers tickle
laughter from celestial verbs.
But here at ground level I shock
the snowfall with tracks easy
to conceal, impossible to heal.

Dawn apparitions flutter
in the fringe of marsh across the road.
I would like to address them
in language that would freeze them
into attention. But I wield
my snow shovel as a weapon.
Only the elder ghosts respond.

Father Snow

Father Snow is more Catholic
than the Pope. When he greets me
in Latin, I cringe with shame
for my atheist manner, slurring
my vowels. The actual fact
of faith never arises. Angels
throb in the innocent sky.
A cloud becomes a face trailing
a beard of curly vapors.
He always asks what color
my easily bruised ego
has assumed that day. He inquires
whether the river shallows
have coughed up any rare shellfish.
His glass eye wanders here and there
while his real one focuses
more firmly than his talons.
His fat old housekeeper
complains that sex with Father Snow
keeps her awake every night,
all night, his appetite sturdy
as a football hero's and honed
by the expertise he gained through
his seminary education
and his adventures amid the nuns.
Every day he shakes my hand
as if we'd never met before.
He smiles a brazen rainbow smile
and always looks so expectant.

I want to explain that the god
he cannibalizes weekly
deplores such public excess
and prefers to lurk in the shade.
I want him to understand that
the groans of organs depress
that one authentic god, the one
I often meet in the coffee shop
where Father Snow rarely goes,
preferring tea at the rectory
with his housekeeper brimming
with adoration as he sips.
That honest god reads the paper,
usually the *New York Times,*
with care and then sighs a pale
chemical sigh that lingers
after he sheds his human form
and returns to the fourth dimension.
He always leaves a generous tip
and a word of advice, often
in a language I don't understand.
Not Latin, Hebrew or Greek.
Not Hindi, Arabic, Chinese.
I should write down those words
phonetically and show them
to Father Snow. But he'd shake
his big fistulous head and note
that everything is true in the clouds,
where the angels he most admires
embrace in gusty passions
we should never express aloud.

The Beard I Grew Last Week

The beard I grew last week didn't suit me, so I peeled it off and tossed it in the trash. Today I met my beard plastered onto the face of a stranger. "Where did you get that fur piece?" I asked. "It crawled onto my face while I was asleep," he says. "I tried to shave it off but it's too tough." "You have to peel it," I explain. He gives it a tug. Nothing. I feel I ought to rescue him, although I don't see how I'm to blame. So I drive him to the hardware store to ask for advice. The clerks gather around and look at the beard. One recommends painter remover. But that's awfully caustic to apply to a face. Another wields a putty knife, but the beard is tougher than old wallpaper. Finally one comes up with a powerful belt sander. The roar of this device is dreadful, but it should be possible to sand off the beard with minimal facial damage. As soon as the vibration touches the beard it drops from the fellow's face and scampers down the aisle. We lose sight of it. Probably the next time anyone sees it, it will be a mouse nest with a dozen pinkies cuddled up for warmth.

Fish Tail

Sometimes after tiring dreams
I awaken with a fish-tail.
A catch in my breath warns me
I belong in a weedy green ocean
with a single perfect horizon.
Going about my daily chores
balanced on a fish tail instead
of legs numbs me more than cycling
forever uphill or teaching
in classrooms of ghostly echoes.
As I shop for fruit and vegetables
or slop up the post office ramp
to collect my daily cache of mail
people notice the fish tail and shake
their heads in pity. At the café
the barista admits that sometimes
he also awakens fish-tailed
with a mermaid snoring beside him.
He stays home from work, however,
until the tail withers and falls off.
I must sleep away my fish-tail
and awaken freshly legged again.
But for a full day I must suffer
amphibious little passions
no earthly mate can satisfy.
Then the sudden winter night
will drape me in its decencies
and I'll dream myself underseas
in a tangle of Sargasso mulch.

The next day I'll rise on my legs,
and except for a few iridescent
scales on the floor no evidence
of my fish-life will remain.

Boulevard by the Sea

You're driving badly today.
On the boulevard by the sea
you hit every pothole and dash
your Mercedes to scrap. On foot,
exposed to the midday glare,
our bodies feel gelatinous:

they no longer seem tailored
to our private or public needs.
Why did you drive so carelessly
with your comfortable, expensive car?
You seemed to aim for every pothole,
and when the wheels fell off

I thought I detected a little smile.
Now you amble like a pea hen.
Nothing of romance, no hint
of Rimbaud on the dusty paths
of Africa, nothing of Thoreau
dead-reckoning cross-country

to the east slope of Wachusett.
Only your usual duck-walk
swinging along despite the heat,
despite the slackening of flesh
that afflicts us equally. The sea
behind a screen of wild roses

gnashes and mutters to itself
without the slightest earthly concern.
Sometimes we glimpse surf curdling
in foam and bathers splashing.
We could descend the few steps
and lie in the sand and roast

ourselves medium rare. But the wreck
of your car by the roadside
would rebuke us, and police
would insist you have it towed away
to discourage others from walking
in this self-digesting heat.

Private and Public

The nineteenth century returns in a gasp of steam and trill of courtship. Passenger pigeons blacken the sky. Pleasure maximizes in a stutter of corsets and stays. Horsehair sofas groan with well-requited sex. Have you ever seen such public affection before? Pink and beige, brown and cream bodies flicker in sunlit rivers where everyone is private and public at once. Do I mean public privates? No, your humor is misplaced. No one laughed in the nineteenth century unless they meant it. You don't mean it. You would never wear a corset. You would never frock yourself in clouds of drapery. Think of Emily Dickinson gardening in the deepest dark, long after the family has gone to bed. Think of Thoreau's moonlit walks, manure squelching under his boots. Where did all those steam engines go? Scrap metal recast in the form of human figures that now dominate. No wonder we feel so tough. No wonder we rust so easily. No wonder no one needs corsets or stays.

Near Bromley

Rain tatters leafless hardwoods.
Shy brooks quicken and surge as
we cross the rough log bridges.
Ahead, the foggy summit deflates
like the Hindenburg, its demise
in misty corrugations of cloud
painless and much to the point.

You laughed when I packed an umbrella,
called me a "gentleman hiker,"
postulated a briefcase crammed
with apples, croissants, and wine
instead of my canvas knapsack
and canteen of ginger beer.
You laughed, but walking side by side

along the tired old trail we're dry
despite the downpour rattling
the fresh brittle leaves underfoot.
They wince as if bullet struck.
Here in southern Vermont the wealth
penetrates even into the woods.
We meet a man equipped by Orvis

with hundred-dollar tweed pants
and shooting jacket, Johnson
and Murphy leather-soled loafers,
a wool flannel shirt, silver hair
dripping, astoundingly drunk.

How did he get here? On his way down,
no doubt, from a much greater height.

Despite his deep inebriation
he's dancing on the slippery rocks.
Perhaps a warped sort of prophet
descending to warn all Vermont
that its mountaintops are failing
to reveal long views to honor
our new obsession with landscape

not as still-life but as drama.
The contours muddle and roil
like pages of sacred text.
The rain-fog's the smoldering ego
that negates the art of creation
for the sake of self-obsession,
driving aged Isaiahs to drink.

Black in Gray America

(In memory of Sam Cornish)

You recalled a city of stinks:
the shabby breath of yellow teeth,
filthy socks on crusty feet,
blood-spill dried on the sidewalk.
The dirt-floor basement room
your mother tried to sweep clean
rustled all night as rodents
named and renamed you in dreams.

The sorry carcass of Baltimore
coughed up feverish gases
that drove you north to Boston
where you rewrote Richard Wright
in tough black-letter alphabets
even the shyest child could read.
When I met you in the Booksmith
I knew that inhaling the pointed dark
and exhaling crystalline spores
wasn't your aesthetic mode.

Over whiskey we bent our brains
to map wood and tarpaper shacks
filled with timid barefoot children
in the gulch between Roxbury
and Jamaica Plain. We offered
ourselves on the bloody fields
of lower education, our ties
strangled and flopping like tongues.

You understood the gangsters
lurking in the corners of our eyes.
You spoke the lone upholstered word
that opened books without cracking
the most fragile, dried-glue spines.
You laughed in the tones of those
for whom the bell tolls, peppering
the streetscape with dust and ashes.

Later, after the children flew
to asbestos-shingled coops,
you cooked by pouring bourbon
into spaghetti sauce and tainting
the mess with the hottest peppers
the inmates of insane asylums
in the Yucatan dared to grow.

More comfortable in the dark
despite the books that lit your lair,
you scrawled plats of the city
of stinks on the backs of your hands.
Farrell and Wolfe, favorite authors,
along with Wright and Baldwin,
enlivened your dullest moments.

When you threated to run away
with a famous white woman poet
I realized how intersected
your world was, how thickly paved.
When you slammed yourself against
the walls of a house in Wayland
and shattered a hundred egos
I clenched myself with remiss.

You knew what you were living.
Being black in gray America
deranged itself while you leaned back
and let movies and comics wash
away the debris, leaving something
I can't identify, stainless
and bold and placed exactly where
no one expects a monument.

You've Taken Up Smoking

You've taken up smoking because
at eighty you've nothing to lose.

A cigarette thrusts from your fist
like an angry little penis.

You want to spend ten dollars
a pack and smoke one butt a day

for the rest of your repentance.
What crime have you committed

that has sentenced you to clog
your lungs with carbon monoxide?

Your hero-poets smoked themselves
into premature deaths that struck

abruptly as a property tax.
Look at the wrinkles Auden grew.

Look at Lowell slumped in a cab,
Bishop flat-out on the carpet.

You smoke with childish defiance
and scatter ashes in your wake.

None of our friends smoke but glare
as you strut about with flaring

equine nostrils, the curls
of smoke offending a cosmos

already tainted with waste.
Why don't you quit while young enough

to enjoy a few balmy seasons
before the dark closes forever?

I won't pay for your cigarettes
but might hire a priest to exorcize

the fire-demon living inside you
with his prickly attitude glooming.

Coleridge's Plagiarisms

Walking at an obtuse angle to the world, I'm disappointed that my shadow doesn't follow me. Granite boulders scruffy with lichen stare with unabashed curiosity. Houses set far apart on ruled lots look aghast. Yet my neighbors understand. I'm the lunatic who always walks little sideways not crab-like but more like a shopping cart with one jammed wheel. I'm obtuse but the world if acute. No wonder it aches so deeply. When I reach the brook at the foot of the hill it's barely flowing. The chatter of current over stone discloses nothing I hadn't already known. The distant rage of a chainsaw tempers the stillness. Someday I'll run amok with a power tool. Not a chin, though—something more compatible with the sloped and reckless geometry of my relationship to landscape. My shadow doesn't understand me, though. It has probably gone home and settled in my old leather chair with a good book. I think it has been reading Coleridge's *Biographia.* Probably mulling over the author's blatant plagiarisms and wishing that it had the nerve to emulate him.

On Inishbofin

Only the sea matters, heavy
with conspicuous lack of passion.
A few sails hack at the gloom.

The ferry has just departed
and we're watching a power shovel,
an orange Hitachi, nose at

a pile of crates full of fish.
A boat squats at the pier. Thick men
grumble in shades of gray no one

but they can interpret. We gaze
at the "hotel and marine spa"
where we're destined to lie awake

through a night of restless seabirds.
The museum and gift shop
opened when the ferry arrived

so we step inside and inhale
a hundred years of mildew.
Once we would have bought postcards

but the Internet has negated
such primitive communication.
With a bag of trinkets selected

for pity's sake we settle outdoors
at the Beach Restaurant and nibble
fish and chips washed down with ale.

Tattered flags racket in the wind.
Why did we abandon the mainland
to gnaw at the shore of an island

we'll never comprehend? We walk
to what the map calls a "photo point"
but see nothing but green-gray swells

and woolen sky, a stone tower
thrust at us like an insult.
The dirt track curves along the shore

and promises to go nowhere so
we surrender to the little hotel
and lie as flat as the bed allows,

hoping the sea won't rise or sky
drape brocades all over us,
mocking our lack of presence.

A Day of Definition

Shadows on whitewashed siding
writhe to reveal the life within
a simple geometric scene.

Sunlight encrusts us watching
angels form and dissolve as
the branches on which they perch

sway in the general elegance.
This scene occurs to us daily,
although we don't always notice

the possibly divine component.
We aren't people of the sun
but of the shallows of darkness

that hide behind all lit objects.
We sulk too deeply to inhale
the massive photons without

coughing and choking in public.
The moving shadows confront us
with the fact of living matter

interacting with self and other.
Do we do that? Do we struggle
to expose evolving tissue

and risk celestial laughter?
The creation hasn't finished
creating us. We sip our coffee

at the general store and consider
how much we've already wrung
from this day of definition.

Even without our witness
we're sure that the bushes laden
with daylight angels revel

in the script they're scrawling on
plank siding that otherwise
would go wordless in the noon.

To a Crustacean

The old car you bought to restore
rusted into pieces small enough
to shovel up and tote to the dump.
The ten children you fathered
with other citizens' wives
matured into a mob that looted
and burned your house to the ground.

Now you rustle in tall grass
and sift for clues. You're too late—
the mystery fled decades ago,
leaving hardly a wisp of spoor.
A dry cough flusters the forest.
A portable generator roars
but barely produces a spark.

Men with power tools attempt
to construct something fresh enough
to survive your battleship outlook.
Manly as the rear of the school bus
where you exposed yourself to girls,
your bulk precedes and follows you
through the unwinding of the mind

that braced you against a critique
handed down by a circuit judge.
You've just inherited the air
that lingered in your mother's house.
But you have no place to store it

except in fingertip memory
reserved for women you found

cranky as snarls of barbed wire.
You're afraid to conflate them
with your mother's sightless love.
But be assured that we're all
a single species: our bloodlines,
like the plumbing of your burned house,
tortured but somehow intact.

On Modern Music

A conference on modern music.
We must sing, not read, our papers.
In your session on Stravinsky
your wobbly alto triumphs
and you earn a spatter of applause.
In my session on Aaron Copland

I shatter into semiquavers
and the audience laughs and exits.
The empty room sighs. Wallpaper
peels in one corner; a dusty
skeleton left over from
a medical symposium gloats.

You've already packed the car
and posted your refreshed vita
online where the powers that be
can savor its plush bibliography.
I'll never admit I was here
and won't try to publish my paper

on *Appalachian Spring* and
its derivation from Hart Crane.
As we drive away, the college
recedes in the rearview mirror,
a glut of institutional brick.
Good thing you're driving, your hands

steady on the wheel. The forces
that broke my voice still linger.

They pool like vapor on the lawns
of timid suburban houses.
What do Copland and Stravinsky
care about our flimsy afterthoughts?

Maybe when we go home my voice
will have recovered its bass notes.
Or maybe I'm destined to simper
through my last years singing chords
shaped like broken knuckles aching
in the aftermath of a brawl

Dimensional Night

The city dark isn't lack of light
but fine black matter dusted
into every available space.

Inhaling it is painless,
but lamplight fails to disperse it.
I park my car near the river.

Two huge gasometers loom
as I walk a long, unlit block
to the avenue where neon

and other garish colors fail
to dent the dimensional night.
No one else visible, shops closed

but bars grumbling and theaters
quivering with heated molecules.
I'd planned to catch a certain film

but it's no longer showing.
The marquee's blank, the box office
an empty coffin. A street sweeper,

a huge yellow machine, trundles
along, raising dust and groaning
as if every throb of its engine

unleashed grating inhuman grief.
I must return to my car and drive
myself to another location

where the dark isn't material
and the streets riot with laughter.
But the side street no longer points

to bulky gasometers posed
against a faint tinge of starlight.
It leads directly to the riverbank,

where I stand and stare at the black
and fluent world and realize
it has concealed me from my life.

Water is Flesh

The innocence of lake and stream
impresses you. Running water,
even windy ripples, conceals
depths you dismiss as casual.
You don't realize that water
is flesh, thinned to a flux.

You can't name all the horrors
salting the mud-bottom, decaying
into matter so uncertain science
can't assay it. Drowned children
whose parents never bothered
to search for them. Wooden boats

sunk and drilled by millions of worms.
Glass, cardboard, plastic. Sewage
and filthy runoff. Grave rocks
under which creation evolves
with distorted ideas of the world.
You wonder why no boaters

skim the choppy surface. No fear
of capsizing keeps them indoors.
They've glimpsed something happening
beneath facile equivocations,
something you don't recognize
as proto-human and desperate.

Streams pour into lakes and bring
their habits with them. One
is Heraclitus' claim that change
is the only constant. Agreed,
but being unable to step
into the same river twice cripples

and burdens the imagination.
Drink the lake one glass at a time,
gently assuaging a healthy thirst.
You realize we're made of water,
but you mustn't be too eager
to embrace and encourage the flow.

Sheltering in Ourselves

The wind is reshaping itself
to avoid fresh expectations.

Snow dishevels the scenery
that had planned a million flowers.

Only April, but already birds
have scouted their brittle estates,

already hundreds of chipmunks
have doggedly scoured the ground.

I'm happy to lie late in bed,
but you want to resurrect antique

flavors, boiling them on ranges
fueled by gas formed underground

before humans evolved. You want
to toss enormous salads

a brontosaurus might admire.
This reiteration of foodstuffs

reacts to a mid-spring snowstorm
as reagents respond to acids.

Such a descant of the spirit
usually occurs near the solstice,

when heat and thunder mingle
to thump out musical metaphors

as we shelter in ourselves.
Today's already awash in sighs.

The political news shocks us,
the bad actors lost in their roles.

The rise in sea level persists,
eroding properties that once

we coveted for long horizons.
Now we'd rather lose perspective

than see how the vanishing point
has cuddled up to our estate.

You're brewing potables that reek
of vinegar strong enough to kill

the most persistent microbes.
The morning looks too humble

to sustain our mutual worries,
so let's step outside in the snow

and wind and lie down and relax
in the season's last refurbishing.

Entering Maine

Entering Maine at an angle,
we note how sadly the rivers flow,
how the mobile homes go adrift.
A railroad crosscuts the scene.
A locomotive drags flatcars
of bundled lumber, the diesel
panting a posthuman dirge.

A sliver of rain, then a village
slits the naked eye and shames us
for the struggle of its citizens
against the politics of poverty.
We haven't been here for years
and probably no one missed us.
I would unfold a map to place us

in this familiar old location
but no one prints paper maps
anymore, no one knows or cares
where they're going. A river
meets the sea without a murmur
of protest. Several couples sitting
under large umbrellas taunt a sky

that doesn't notice them guzzling
bottled beer to wash down clam
or lobster rolls. Too dramatic
to incorporate into the scene,
the lumber train lumbers along

a few yards from the clam shack.
We've seen enough. We drive on,

the highway rumpled like our clothes,
even the smallest houses aloof.
We thought we might retire to Maine,
but the expense discouraged us
along with the breath of creatures
panting in the pine forests sprawled
over a thousand unmarked graves.

We should recross the border
to New Hampshire and regroup
our senses. Then re-enter Maine
at a more obtuse angle to prove
our innocence, our smiles reflected
in tidepools gnashing pebbles
like evolving mouthfuls of teeth.

The Next-to-the-Last Poem About Religion

On Sundays an ivory distance
interposes between heaven
and earth. Organs masticate
the cosmos, but note by note

fail to pry open the black box
in which our vital data resides.
Hovering over the *Times*
with its archaic pages fluttering

in the summer breeze I sense
the news colluding with gasps
of religious ecstasy. The dead
in terrorist bombings gape

with unanswered questions stark
on their faces. A photograph
of a beleaguered politician
exposes a mind as raw as squash.

If I attended church and prayed
to the most recent apparition
maybe the glare of July
wouldn't cast such ugly shadows.

Or maybe some public healing
would include me in its vast
pharmacology, clotting my pores
with complimentary aloe

and straightening my crooked joints.
But I doubt that a hymn or two,
however badly sung, would convey
the sincerity to excuse me

from the agony of human news.
But maybe that ivory distance
sufficiently insulates me
from the oceanic feeling

Doctor Freud thought I should fear.
Maybe a second cup of coffee
will drug me to process the news
without taking it personally—

my private infamy inert
to the censure of religion,
untouched by the photophobia
of spotting the actual divine.

Acute and Obtuse Angles

Another day of acute
and obtuse angles dueling.

Rain sozzles the village view.
We agree that cosmic forces

distilled from old comic books
have revised the gray perspectives

to account for changes in taste.
You suspect that California

will eventually crumble with drought
and spill millions of citizens

into the ocean where they'll drift
until minesweepers rescue those

still undigested by sharks.
I'm certain that New England

in an era of rising water will
rumple with newborn fjords.

Why do we torture ourselves
with cruel scenarios when friends

are birthing children shaped
like pottery, their brittle cries

referring to fresh imperatives?
We should indulge in their indulgence,

coo over little forms, pet
every passing dog. The treble

of weather mustn't dissuade us.
The wrinkles we earned by teaching

three unteachable generations
mustn't discourage our lust

for the finer points of view.
Those include standing on rocks

by the river, watching the current
ruffle past. Also climbing

the hill in the graveyard to enjoy
autumn hills rimming the lake.

We meet at acute and oblique
angles at once, and anchor ourselves

to a vanishing point created
by an artist we greatly admire.

www.ingramcontent.com/pod-product-compliance
Lightning Source LLC
LaVergne TN
LVHW091057150826
845673LV00002B/609